contents

D1634585

The author is grateful to the following for
illustrations in this book: Alison Rutherford
(III lower, XVIII, XXII, XXIII top, XXV left);
Andrew Birley (front cover, IX, X top, XVII);
John Cooper (VI and XXIV); Charles Anderson
(XV lower); Dept. Photography, Newcastle
University (XIII lower); and Graham Sumner (XX).
The remaining illustrations are those of the author.

Hadrian's Wall is regarded as one of the finest surviving remains of antiquity. Rightfully it has been designated as a World Heritage site, and its setting in the beautiful and unspoiled upland countryside of Northern Britain enhances the attraction.

Constructed between A.D. 120 and 128, the complex of frontier installations ran from sea to sea, over 73 miles long, with an extension down the Cumbrian coast and numerous support forts on both sides of the barrier. It was a testimony to the Roman Government's ability to defy the natural geography and political boundaries. For nearly 300 years, Britain was to possess an awesome artificial frontier.

It matters not that its cost probably far outweighed its effectiveness, or that its real purpose was as much to occupy the energies of the Roman army as to combat a political threat, real or imaginary. The Romans had already been in occupation of the subsequent Wall area since A.D. 80, and the remains of the earlier frontier system are now inextricably interwoven with the later structures.

Today the old Roman frontier serves as a permanent reminder of the glory that was Rome: still something of an enigma and a continuing challenge to archaeologists and historians, a nuisance to farmers and developers, and a much loved attraction for visitors.

Much of the great frontier has disappeared from view, ravaged by centuries of plundering for its stone, obliterated by modern developments, or simply encumbered by the inexorable growth of nature.

This booklet gives a brief introduction to ten of the best sites to visit, all in the beautiful central sector of the Wall, between Lanercost on the Irthing in the west, and Corbridge on the Tyne in the east. This is Hadrian's Wall in its finest setting, where the remains can be inspected and enjoyed at leisure.

Five of the ten sites have substantial visitor services, where much additional information can be obtained, but all possess distinctive and varying remains of the once great frontier.

The Wall in its superb Northumbrian setting

The Power of Rome: hard currency. Bronze coins from recent excavations at Vindolanda.

Early Forts, and part of the Wall, were constructed with turf and timber, as here with the Vindolanda replicas.

Birdoswald is the only site in this booklet situated beyond the borders of Northumberland, which reflects more upon the changes in the landscape and environment than anything else.

Formerly a part of the Henley estate, and with Heritage Memorial Fund support now owned by Cumbria County Council, the fort and civilian settlement stood on the spur of high land above the river Irthing, close to the Willowford bridge which carried the Wall across the river.

Long stretches of the Wall have been preserved on both sides of the fort, together with a milecastle overlooking the bridge site. Until very recently only fine sections of the fort wall and some gateways could be seen, but excavation has now revealed the massive third century granaries. It is known from excavations in the 1920's that the walls of some internal buildings still stand six feet high below the grass. Judging from the mounds in the field to the east, the civilian settlement will also be well preserved.

The farm-house and hemmels stand within the fort platform, and Cumbria County Council has created the nucleus of a small interpretive centre within them. A walk or drive to the west of the fort, towards Banks Turret and the red sandstone Lanercost Priory, is a rewarding experience.

The imposing east gateway at Birdoswald

One of the recently excavated granaries near the farmhouse

The fort of Carvoran stood on a level plateau overlooking the Tipalt burn, with long views to the south and west, and with the famous Nine Nicks of Thirlwall rising to the east. The site remains covered in grass, but in the course of stone robbing and late nineteenth century excavation it produced more inscribed stones than any other Wall fort. It was once the base for a Cohort of Syrian Archers, the only such specialist force amongst the frontier garrison.

The farm buildings of Carvoran form the nucleus of the Roman Army Museum, featuring extensive displays devoted to both the Roman Army and Hadrian's Wall. These provide an excellent introduction to the history of the Northern frontier. There are video programmes about the wall and animated displays, including a large model of a complete fort. The Museum promotes a programme of reconstructional archaeology, in which modern craftsmen use ancient techniques to reconstruct Roman armour and equipment. The displays are constantly changing, as new information comes to light.

Unlike many of these Wall sites, the Roman Army Museum has both easy access from its car park and ample space, making it an ideal place both for those who find walking difficult and those who seek shelter from the elements.

The superb Walltown Crags sector of the Wall is within six hundred yards of the Museum. It is a very evocative stretch of the frontier, with the Wall in all its guises — excavated and preserved, and standing six feet and more in height; excavated and unconserved, crumbling on the onslaught of sheep and the weather; unexcavated and grass covered; and, sadly in some lengths, removed altogether by the whinstone quarry companies, as they profited from the demands for road chippings.

This is the place to contemplate on the problems faced by the masons and labourers who had to build the Wall. How did they haul their supplies up to some of those craggy working areas? And what did the Wall planners really expect to happen in this part of the frontier? The miles and miles of swampy moorlands and forest stretch as far as the eye can see to the north, to the modern border with Scotland and beyond that — an impossible route for any armed force contemplating an assault on the south. One suspects that the builders knew full well that here they were not engaged on a very practical exercise.

The Wall weaves along the crest of the crags at Walltown

The energies of the Northumberland National Parks Department have turned a disaster into a very pleasant site for visitors at Cawfields. Some may like to walk here from Walltown Crags, following the line of the Wall, through the sad remains of Great Chesters fort, but there is an ample car park at the site.

The quarry companies have obliterated another section of the Wall, but the site has been reclaimed to create the attractive parking area alongside the deep pool. Close by is Milecastle 42, lying very uncomfortably on the ridge, the base for a patrol garrison. Observe the extraordinary position of its north gateway, with impossible access for vehicles. One wonders at the inflexibility of the planners who ignored the more sensible site a few yards to the west.

From a high point on the rock to the west of the milecastle you can see what is probably the best of all views of the Vallum, running as straight as a die into the distance to the east. The effects of time have softened its profile today, but once it formed a formidable barrier to the military zone, rendering the theft of military stores a difficult operation for devious natives. We tend to give all our admiration to the Wall masons, but we should not forget the monumental labour of those who had to dig the Wall ditch and the Vallum. For much of the line, they had to toil through whinstone rock or bog, and it would be hard to say which of these was the most unpleasant.

Cawfields Milecastle

The Wall in winter, on Walltown Crags

Beyond Cawfields the Wall follows the crest of the undulating whinsill, past the highest point of Whinshields Crags, to Steel Rigg. This is the name given to the shelter belt of trees which encloses another National Parks car park, at a convenient place to see the most photographed part of the Wall.

To the east there is a breathtaking walk of an hour or so to Housesteads fort, but the term 'breathtaking' is used in its fullest sense, and it should not be attempted by the unfit or ill-shod. To the south-east, Vindolanda can be reached in half an hour.

The Wall on either side of Steel Rigg has been excavated and conserved and although it is not very high today, it does show a particularly brutal stretch which presented considerable building problems. It is also a good place to forget about those ancient stories which spoke of Romans driving chariots along the Wall — without steps on the rampart walk, the angle of the walk would do justice to the Cresta run.

East of Steel Rigg, approaching Crag Lough

The view from Steel Rigg car park, to the east

Approaching Housesteads Fort

XI

Vindolanda lies a mile to the south of the Wall, on the Roman road known as the Stanegate. It was built some 40 years before Hadrian ordered work to start on his new frontier, and it was one of several forts, such as Carlisle, Nether Denton and Corbridge, which housed the earlier garrison. It was then re-built and became a Wall fort, like Carvoran, in spite of being physically detached from the barrier.

It was a well chosen site, on a level plateau above the junction of two streams, and close to major deposits of iron, lead, clay, stone and coal.

The replicas of the Wall

Now owned by a registered charity, Vindolanda has become a permanent research establishment, and the scene of some of the most exciting excavations in the former Roman World. Both the absence of serious modern destruction and the astonishing preservative properties of the soil have contributed to the survival of even the most fragile of Roman materials. The Museum, equipped with its own laboratory, has the largest collections of leather goods, textiles and wooden objects of any site in the former Roman Empire. But one room is devoted to a photographic display of the most precious of all finds, the fragile documents and correspondence. Written on specially prepared thin sheets of wood, these are the earliest written records from Britain, dating to the years A.D. 90-125. In their own words the soldiers and wives of commanding officers tell us of their lives on the northern frontier of the Roman Empire, in a period for which we have no other surviving records.

On the site the remains of one of the stone forts and civilian buildings outside its walls can be seen, and the military bath-house and the large

The headquarters building of the Fourth Cohort of Gauls

The Baths Suite of the Mansio

mansio or inn for travellers are particularly fine — as is the headquarters building in the fort. But Vindolanda has a hidden underworld, deep down below the stone buildings. There are in places 20 feet of Roman debris, with the remains of as many as eight buildings on top of each other. The earliest five were built of wood, and the posts, beams and planks still remain in good condition, visible only when excavations are in progress.

Dominating the southern part of the field are the huge replicas, sections of Hadrian's Wall in both turf and stone. They show how massive the Wall once was, and they remind the visitors that the western section of the Wall was first built of turf. Their construction, in 1972-74, gave a valuable insight into the logistics of Wall building.

Vindolanda, from the east

Housesteads is the best known of all the forts on the Wall, thanks to its inaccessibility to stone robbers and to the excavations of the late nineteenth century and more recent times. It is a superb site for one of Britain's best-known ancient monuments, perched on the crest of the Northumbrian whinsill ridge, amidst stimulating upland scenery. It is doubtful, however whether the Roman garrison, a thousand strong, appreciated the site as much as modern visitors.

Owned by the National Trust and administered by English Heritage, Housesteads is today the most complete example of a Roman fort to be seen anywhere within the bounds of the former Empire, although its excavation is far from finished. Careful early twentieth-century restoration of the damaged fort walls have much improved the flavour of the place, although the tiny museum, constructed in the 1930's as 'a shelter for visitors in inclement weather' does not do justice to the magnificence of the site.

On the way up to the fort — a rather longer walk from the car park than many people imagine — a number of civilian buildings can be seen, and the south gate possesses an additional feature in the shape of a border reiver's stronghold. Inside the fort the superb latrine building must not be missed — as fine an example of Roman sanitary engineering as anything else in Britain — and the granaries, the headquarters building and commanding officer's house are all fully excavated. Unusually, Housesteads possessed a hospital block, which has also been excavated, and some of the sadly damaged barracks can be seen.

There are first class walks in all directions from Housesteads, and especially along the Wall to east and west. But when it is blowing a gale and pouring with rain, do not forget that the Roman soldiers had the benefit of roofs on their buildings, with warm fires burning in the hearths. It certainly was a much more uncomfortable posting than nearby Vindolanda, but at least it had the views denied to a dreary site like Carrawburgh.

The finest Roman Latrine in Britain

The view to the south from the Commanding Officer's Residence

The north gateway of nearby Milecastle 37, with blocking wall

CARRAWBURGH

This was arguably the most unpleasant posting on Hadrian's Wall. The fort lay on a windswept moor, surrounded by soggy marshes, with the most tedious of views in all but the southerly direction. The spacious car park alongside the road promises much, but the fort, badly robbed by the eighteenth century road-builders, has little beyond coarse grazing for sheep. But there is a fine Wall treasure here to see, hidden below the south-western corner of the fort.

In the late nineteenth century Carrawburgh swept to prominence with the discovery of the temple to Coventina alongside the small stream to the west of the fort, and the magnificent haul of votive tablets, altars and coins gave notice to the interested public that the wet soils of Northumberland still preserved a vast amount of Roman material. Today the shrine of Coventina is sadly neglected, overgrown with marsh grass and reeds, and few visitors ever find it.

But a few yards to the south lies the compact little temple of Mithras, discovered in 1949, and well preserved for inspection. The altars and the wattle fencing are well disguised replicas, and you have to visit the Museum of Antiquities in Newcastle to see the real things. But as an example of what can still survive, the tiny Mithraic temple should be inspected, for it will always act as a spur to those with the knowledge and the ability to undertake further research on Hadrian's Wall.

The Temple to Mithras at Carrawburgh

There is something of a conspiracy to keep visitors away from this marvellous place, and various public bodies have been arguing for years about the necessity or otherwise for a decent car park nearby.

But it is possible to reach it, either by parking in the little lay-by just to the west of the sharp bend at the crest of a hill, or on the verge of the minor road leading off to the north, half a mile to the east. Those who make the effort will be rewarded with some classic views of the frontier.

Blackcarts is the name given to the length of preserved Wall running parallel to the military road as it comes up the hill from the Tower Tye crossroads, and just beyond that, on the summit of the hill, is Limestone Corner. At this point, the most northerly on the Wall, the great Wall ditch lies immediately north of the road, and the equally massive Vallum ditch is on the south, with little more than thirty yards separating them. The Wall is unexcavated at this point.

The remains of the Wall ditch are remarkable. Here it had to be cut through the living whinstone rock, and the sight of the massive chunks lying both on the berm and in the bottom of the ditch are silent witnesses to the gruesome effort required by those long departed Roman labourers. But equally visible today, just to the east of the deepest section of the ditch, is the unmistakable sign that some Roman commander had the courage to ignore the Wall blueprint and call a halt to the unnecessary work, for the fully excavated section gives way to another where only the top-soil and clay had been removed, and then another where little more than the turf had gone.

The ditch diggers are the unsung heroes of the construction gangs: their tasks were far more laborious and boring than those of the Wall builders, yet their efforts perhaps have had a more lasting effect upon the environment today, as farmers make long detours to drive their tractors round the ever present obstacle.

The unfinished Wall ditch, cutting through the living rock at Limestone Corner

The cavalry fort of Chesters lay in the sort of place that a Cistercian monk would certainly have appreciated, in the rich meadowland alongside the North Tyne River, well protected from the fierce winds which can make life difficult on the high whinsill sites. The Wall was brought across the river on a massive bridge, whose southern abutment, with mill race, can be inspected by those prepared to make a lengthy detour by the footpath on the southern side of the modern bridge.

Chesters is an English Heritage site, with appropriate services and staffing, and it contains a unique little museum, constructed and laid out at the beginning of this century. Within its cramped space there is the most comprehensive collection of Roman inscriptions to be found anywhere in Britain, brought together and preserved by the Clayton family in the nineteenth century. Many of the best stones from Carvoran, Great Chesters, Housesteads, Vindolanda, and Carrawburgh can be found here, alongside Chesters' own contributions.

The outstanding remains here are those of the ornate headquarters building, the commanding officer's residence, some partially excavated barrack buildings, and the military bath-house, nestling against the bank alongside the river.

The military bath-house on the north bank of the North Tyne

It is unfortunate, although not surprising, that the obvious quality of this site was recognised by later builders, and the presence of the Chesters mansion alongside the fort inhibits further excavation and display. But Chesters has enormous potential for the future, with the opportunity for archaeologists to excavate a complete cavalry fort with its large civilian settlement.

The difference between a posting to a site like this compared with, say Carrawburgh or Housesteads, is marked, for although all the forts were but a part of the same frontier system, no two of them lay in the same environment.

Cavalry Barracks at Chesters

Corbridge, generally known by the corrupt Roman name Corstopitum, but probably really Coria, was not a Wall fort. Its origins, like those of Carvoran and Vindolanda, go back to the first years of Roman occupation. Situated on the north bank of the Tyne, close to a ford and later the major Roman bridge, Corbridge sat astride the north-south highway, stretching from York to Scotland. It was therefore, like Carlisle, always a key strategic site, and it was to develop into the Wall region's second largest town.

The visible remains are but a small part of the site, and much excavation was undertaken in the surrounding fields during the intensive campaign of the early twentieth century. Many of the finds from that work can be inspected in the new museum, which finally succeeded a variety of long lived temporary structures in 1983.

Some of the visible remains are difficult for even the initiated to unravel, as walls of different periods are all preserved together, especially on the south side. As there are numerous changes to the plans and a long occupation, later stone walls can be seen subsiding into inadequately sealed earlier ditches and pits. Like Vindolanda, Corbridge has a great depth of occupation material.

There are some outstanding buildings to inspect. The great twin granaries close to the Museum are probably the best of their kind in Britain, and the column bases to the south of them, near the huge watertank, would not look out of place at Pompeii. To the east lies the enormous building known as Site XI, apparently never completed, but making use of some of the most imposing masonry to be seen anywhere. It was perhaps designed as a town Forum, when the emperor Severus had grand plans for the north, but his death at York in 211 saw the abandonment of his new impetus.

The site guidebook will help you locate the small legionary compounds to the south of the main road, which include a mini headquarters building, with an underground strongroom.

Corbridge was the first frontier site to attract the attention of treasure hunters, when King John used his army to dig for gold and silver. Sadly his example is still followed by some of those with metal detectors, as they risk prosecution for the sake of Roman finds.

The massive masonry of the enigmatic Site XI

The south front of a Granary alongside the main road

The excavated and preserved remains of buildings are only the empty symbols of a garrison which watched over the northern frontier of the Roman Empire for three hundred years. We can inspect those remains and we can watch as archaeologists slowly reveal more of the vast frontier complex. But if we want to find out what life was like for those soldiers and civilians, we have to turn to a most complex patchwork of sources.

The accidents of survival have denied to us the bulk of what Roman historians had to say about the history of the province and we are left with only fragmentary and sometimes contradictory statements. But other parts of the Empire, and other frontier regions, are better documented, and we are entitled to assume that the garrison on the northern frontier behaved in much the same way as its colleagues did on the Rhine or the Danube

— or even in North Africa and Egypt. It was, after all, the same Roman Army which maintained the peace throughout the far flung Empire.

In the Wall Museums you will be able to see the personal possessions of the men and women who once inhabited the forts and civilian settlements. The armour and weapons, the tools and equipment, the domestic utensils and pottery, the jewellery and coins all portray a society whose material resources were far in advance of any which their successors possessed for many centuries. And because Roman society was literate, we also have many of their building inscriptions, altars and tombstones, which at least give us the names of men and women, with some information about their activities.

The bronze horse from Vindolanda, possibly from a military standard

Jet Betrothal Medallion

But the greatest source of information has only recently come to light. The wooden writing tablets from Vindolanda and Carlisle have suddenly shown us that the potential for a dramatic improvement in our knowledge of that garrison is at hand. The buildings may be no more than shattered foundations, and their occupants material possessions may be broken and fragmentary, but the letters and accounts,

A Birthday Party Invitation for Sulpicia Lepidina, circa A.D. 100

Damaged in transit — pottery from southern Gaul dumped in a fort ditch at Vindolanda circa A.D. 90

military orders and lists can make up for the deficiencies in a most vivid manner.

It is clear that the Roman army on garrison duty on this frontier behaved in a similar manner to modern armies engaged in the same function. Most of the time was spent on training, fetching and distributing supplies, repairing or renewing buildings and equipment, and the host of daily chores which any organisation has to undertake. The correspondence from Vindolanda never mentions offensive action against the natives, although it must have occurred from time to time, and only once are the locals recorded at all, being referred to as *Brittunculi* or wretched Britons.

Even in the pre-Hadrianic days, there was the opportunity for Commanding officers wives to engage in social visits to each other and to devote themselves to the well being of their children who were with them. Leave was being applied for on a regular basis, and probably granted, and a host of official duties could result in only a small proportion of a regiment actually being present at their fort. At one time, circa A.D. 90, a strength report of the First Cohort of Tungrians at Vindolanda tells of more than 470 men and five centurions being absent and of the remaining 275 or so men, over 30 were listed as being unfit for duty. It is not an untypical picture for a modern regiment.

We should not therefore regard the frontier garrison as being a static force, grimly defending their forts against a determined enemy. It is probably closer to the truth to accept that many an auxiliary soldier spent his 25 years service without ever casting his spear in anger. The worst violence he faced was probably the punishment regularly meted out by his centurion for a variety of offences, as in the case of the unfortunate and un-named Vindolanda soldier, who complained both that he was innocent and that as a man from overseas he did not deserve the lashing he had received. Presumably he regarded beatings as being more appropriate for recruits drawn from the Britons.

Although in the early days only senior officers would have been able to have their families with them, by the third century the situation was very different. The growth of civilian settlements outside the fort walls led to a substantial civilian population being attached inexorably to the garrison, with numerous soldiers families, merchants and others. By that stage garrisons did not change so frequently, and life for the soldiers became much closer to that of modern soldiers in a garrison town.

Replica of a Roman Chamfron — the decorative head guard of a cavalry horse

The ten sites in this booklet all lie within 25 miles of each other in the beautiful central sector of the Wall. The combination of evocative remains and lovely setting is unmatched by anything elsewhere, but there are other places which contain excellent Wall material.

In modern South Shields, at the mouth of the Tyne, the remains of the large stores base and fort are displayed, together with a small site Museum and the magnificent replica fort gateway. At Newcastle University, in the heart of the City, the Museum of Antiquities contains a good display of finds from the Wall, especially inscribed stones. At the other side of the country, in Carlisle, the newly refurbished Tullie House Museum contains some of the best material from the western sector.

Elsewhere, as the Ordnance Survey Map of Roman Britain will show you, there is a multitude of Roman remains, largely unexcavated, belonging to support forts of the frontier. Some lie well to the north of the wall line, like Risingham, near West Woodburn on the A68, or lonely Bewcastle, north of Birdoswald; others lie on the Roman roads through the Pennines, or down the west coast.

Gold finger ring, with gemstone featuring Medusa

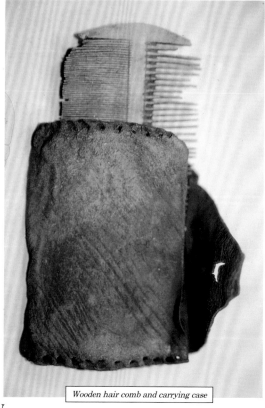

Wooden hair comb and carrying case

£2.50